INTERMEDIATE JAZZ PIANO COMPING

"At The Bridge"

By Tom Anderson

Can be used separately or in conjunction with:
Playing Guitar In A Big Band
and
Groove Master: Playing Drum Set in a Jazz Rhythm Section
and
I Walk The Line: Creating a Bass Line for the Beginning Jazz/Big BandBass Player

Houston
PUBLISHING, INC.
DISTRIBUTED BY
HAL•LEONARD
CORPORATION
7777 W. BLUEMOUND RD. P.O. BOX 13819 MILWAUKEE, WI 53213

About The Author

Tom Anderson has a degree in music from Minot (ND) State University, the University of North Texas, and the University of Missouri-Kansas City. He has played bass in a number of jazz ensembles including the jazz choir, Connection, at the University of Missouri-Kansas City which was directed by Kirby Shaw. He taught at the Schuylkill Campus of Penn State University and Eastern Washington University. Dr. Anderson continues to be active as a performer as well as a composer/arranger with pieces published by Houston Publishing, Inc., CPP/Belwin, Word Music, Somerset Press, and the University of Northern Colorado Jazz Press.

Table of Contents

Chapter 1: A Review of the Basics

Playing piano in a jazz group is a challenging adventure. You are expected to provide (as a minimum) the "correct" harmony for a composition. The "clues" that you are given are chord symbols which are listed above the melody. It is your responsibility to interpret them properly and add interesting notes to the given chord.

This book is designed as a sequel to Jazz Piano Comping for the Beginning Jazz Improvisor. If you find that you do not understand the material in this volume, you may want to review the first book which is designed as a "beginning" for all jazz piano compers.

The subtitle for the first book is "From the Top." This is a jazz term which means the beginning of a composition (or CHART). This book's subtitle is "At the Bridge." The BRIDGE is a portion of music that usually occurs after the first section of a composition. It is used for contrast before the music returns to the first material.

Sometimes the bridge can be more difficult than the first part of a piece. This can be in terms of a more advanced harmony or intricate melody. Jazz compositions such as "One Note Samba," "Take Five," or "Body and Soul" have bridges that could be viewed as more complex than the opening sections. So if you are ready for more advanced jazz harmony, this book is for you.

As a jazz piano comper you are expected to improvise the rhythm of the accompaniment. You must decide which notes are to be played (harmony) as well as the rhythmic content. Most of the suggested chords in the song samples will be written using quarter, half, or whole notes. Unless the composition is a ballad do not use notes of long duration when creating a piano accompaniment. The piano is a percussive instrument. Use that quality when playing pieces that have medium to fast tempos.

One essential rhythmic aspect of most jazz pieces is the treatment of the eighth note. If words like "Swing," "Shuffle," or " Jazz Feel" are written at the beginning of an arrangement to describe the rhythm, eighth notes are not equal. They are played as:

The first eighth note in a set of two is longer than the second. Therefore, a group of four eighth notes would be played like this:

There is a feeling of "long-short, long-short" when playing eighth notes in a jazz pieces. It will take some time to adjust to this rhythmic feeling but it should become natural after a time.

Some arrangers write swing eighth notes as dotted eighth notes followed by sixteenth notes. They would not be played as written but converted to triplet division.

Fortunately, most arrangers do not write swing eighth notes in this manner. If they were played as dotted eighth notes and sixteenth notes, they would sound very "square."

Chapter 2: Chord Construction and Symbols

As a pianist you are probably familiar with chords. A CHORD is three or more notes played at the same time. Here is a C major chord.

You will rarely play this chord as written in a jazz setting. Jazz harmony is quite advanced and a chord this simply constructed would sound out of place.

But you do need to understand the basic construction of chords before you attempt to add "interesting" notes to them. Again, if you find this material too advanced refer back to the book Jazz Piano Comping for the Beginning Jazz Improvisor.

The letter "C" written above the previous example is a CHORD SYMBOL. These are a series of letters and numbers that appear above the music. They provide a method of musical shorthand that is very common in jazz. By using chord symbols, composers and arrangers expect musicians to have the ability to interpret them and play the appropriate notes at the correct time.

Each type of chord will be discussed in detail before they are used in song samples. Here is an overview of the three most widely used types of chords in jazz (and much popular music as well): major, minor, and dominant. You may want to refer back to this information once you are playing chords in the examples. The chords are first illustrated with the minimum number of notes.

Major Chords

One of the most common types of chords is MAJOR. A C major chord was illustrated for the idea of a chord. The chord symbol for a major chord is a letter which represents the ROOT of the chord or its lowest note in this example.

The other two notes of a major chord are the THIRD and FIFTH.

As a jazz pianist you should be familiar with the construction of each chord type. Initially, you will probably be concerned with "what notes are in each chord." Eventually you will want to add notes for a more authentic jazz sound.

One method of achieving this authenticity is to spread the notes of the chord so you play with a more "open" sound. Here, a C major chord is represented by two VOICINGS (a combination of notes that suggest a chord).

You are probably noticing a few things. The root of the chord is not the bottom note (it is the bass player's responsibility to play this note). The three notes of a C major chord (C, E, and G) are present in the first voicing but not the second (there is no C). The notes D and A are added to the first voicing and D, A, and B are added to the second. Hopefully, you are also noticing that these voicings sound "good" and "jazzy."

Minor Chords

The next most common type of chord is MINOR. While a major chord has a "happy" or "jovial" sound, a minor chord sounds "sad" or "somber."

Here are some possible chord symbols for a D minor chord. The letter representing the root is followed by a "-," "m," "mi," or "min" as the chord symbol for a minor chord. Each of these chord symbols represent the same chord.

D- Dm Dmi Dmin

Here are the three notes that make up this chord. Again, each note is either the root, third, or fifth of a D minor chord.

By adding the appropriate notes you can play "authentic" jazz voicings. Each of these chords will be illustrated when they are used in a song sample.

Dominant Chords

The third most common type of chord is DOMINANT. It has a quality of unrest and has the feeling it needs to "go" some place for harmonic "stability." While these chords have a certain amount of dissonance and tension, they are very common in popular music (particularly in rock and roll).

Here is a G dominant seventh chord. The chord symbol for any dominant type of chord is a letter which represents the root followed by a number (7, 9, 11, or 13).

G7 G9 G11 G13

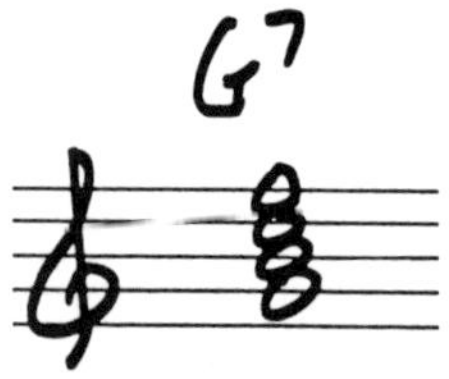

A dominant seventh chord has four notes while a major or minor chord has only three. The fourth note is called the Seventh.

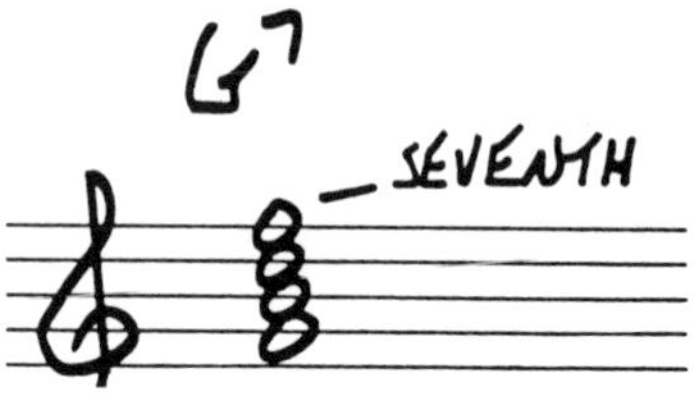

Each of these notes do not have to be included in a dominant chord voicing. Again, the bassist will usually play the root (G) so that note does not have to be present.

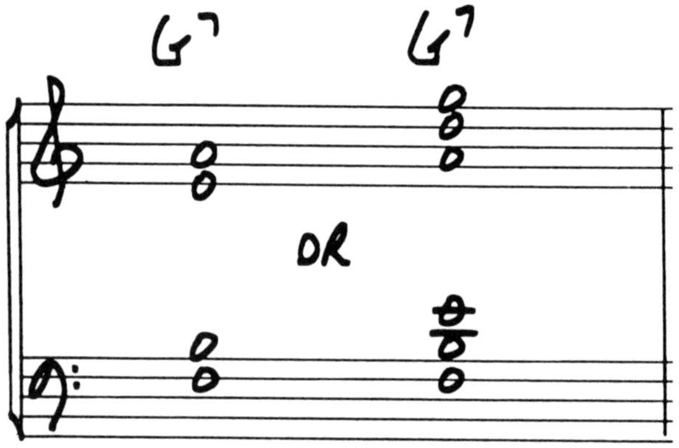

These are appropriate voicings even when "G7" is the chord symbol. The added notes (A, E, or D) enhance the "jazz" quality and are commonly included for a G7 chord.

Even though the chord families of major, minor, and dominant do not represent all of the chords you will play in a jazz composition, the vast majority of chords are one of these types. You should develop the ability to analyze the chord symbols.

Actually, you may be surprised by how few notes you have to play to get an authentic jazz sound. You can play the "important" notes of each chord (third, fifth, or seventh) and add one or two pitches. This will be enough for the rich harmony of most jazz pieces.

Chapter 3: Minor Chord Progressions

A CHORD PROGRESSION is a series of chords played one after another. You continue to play the same chord until another is indicated.

When reading music for jazz performances, chords are written above the staff which will contain the melody, suggested voicings, or an actual piano accompaniment with specified rhythm.

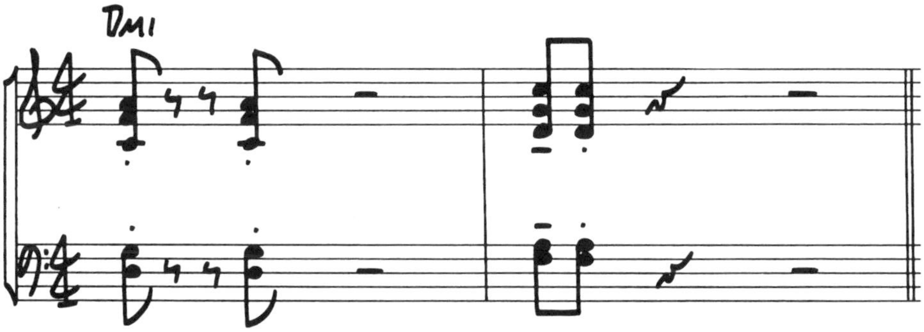

Feel free to improvise an accompaniment if you think you can improve the musical performance by doing so. Each of these notational systems serves as a guide to be used for your interpretation.

In the next example the piano part is specified. This would be an "authentic" comping pattern if the bass part was played on another instrument such as a string bass or bass guitar.

EXERCISE 1

(note: All exercises are correlated to Playing Guitar in a Big Band, I Walk The Line, and Groove Master: Playing Drum Set in a Jazz Rhythm Section. They can be played by yourself or with the other members of a rhythm section.)

It is your challenge to improvise this type of accompaniment when only a chord symbol is given.

Now the chord progression moves from a D minor chord to a G dominant seventh. Again, assume that the bass part is played on another instrument.

EXERCISE 2

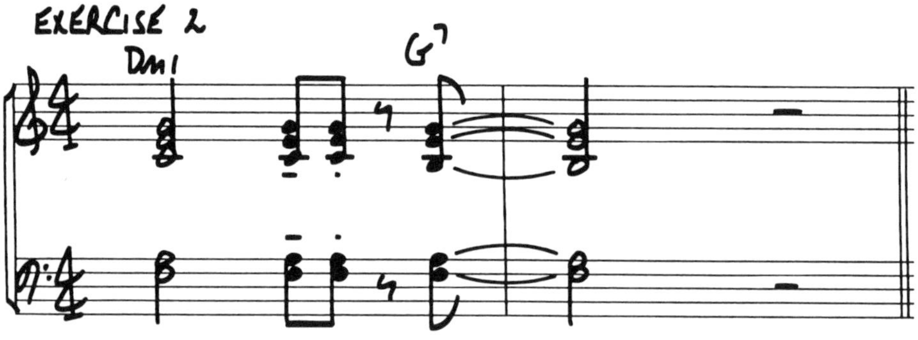

In most jazz pieces there will be at least one chord for each measure. Many jazz chord progressions have two or more chords in a measure so you move quickly from chord to chord. Your eventual goal is to move smoothly from chord to chord selecting the appropriate notes and adding some "interesting" ones as well.

While most jazz compositions have many chords, that is not the case with "Illusions." It only has two chords and they are the same chord type (minor) a half step apart.

A composition such as this offers a challenge to an accompanying player because it is their responsibility to make it "interesting." But how can you do so with only two chords in the progression (and they are the same type of chord)?

This is a good example of the necessity to add the appropriate notes to a chord. It would be boring to simply shift from a D minor to an Eb minor chord using only the notes of each chord (D, F, A and Eb, Gb, Bb, respectively).

While the material from Jazz Piano Comping for the Beginning Jazz Improvisor could be thought of as: "what notes does each chord symbol represent," this book describes "what notes can be added to the chords."

It is a lifelong endeavor to come up with interesting accompaniments so this is just the preliminary step. Again, please feel free to refer to the first book if you do not understand the basics of reading chord symbols.

Whenever a minor chord is indicated you can usually play a minor seventh chord.

Most jazz chords have at least four notes. It is quite rare to play a triad when creating a jazz piano accompaniment.

The previous chord represents TERTIAN harmony. This is where a chord is built in a series of thirds (either major or minor).

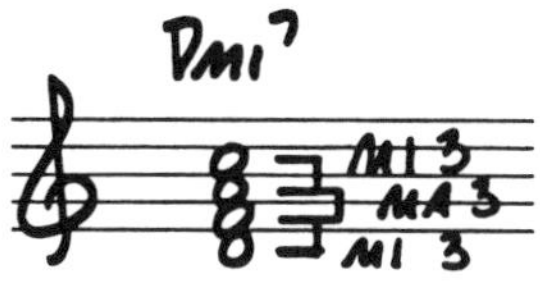

While each of these notes are part of a D minor seventh chord, this is not a very interesting jazz piano voicing. One alternative is to spread the notes out so that there is "space" between the pitches. The greatest space (largest interval) should occur in the lower part of the voicing.

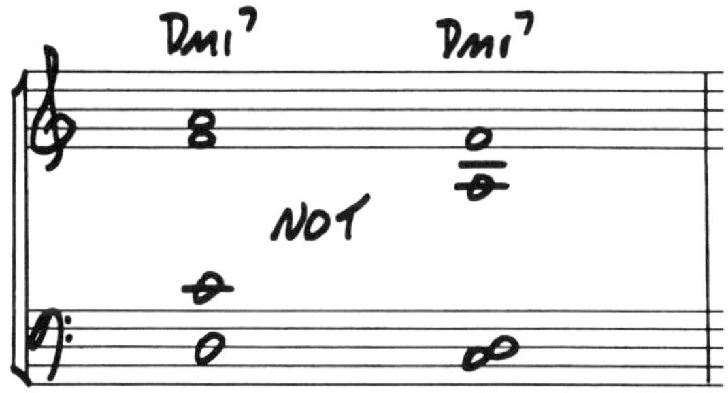

By adding one note (the eleventh) it is easy to create QUARTAL harmony which is much more common for jazz piano. This is where it is a fourth between most of the pitches.

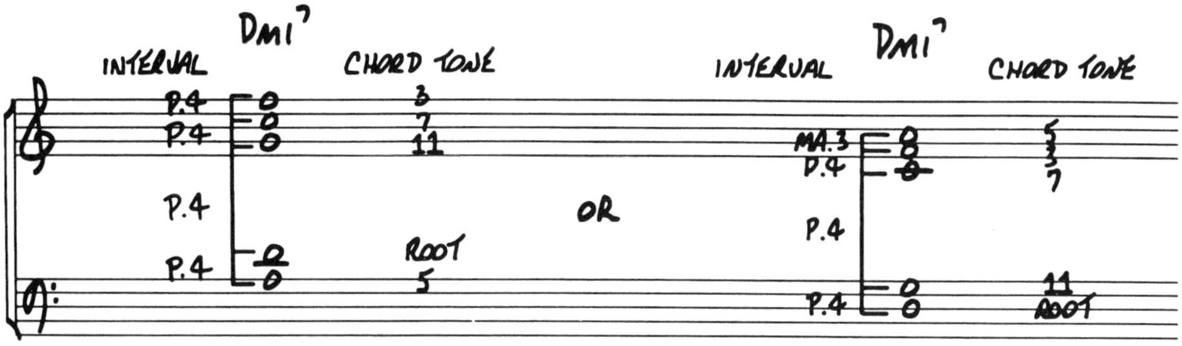

Notice that none of the chords tones are doubled. Also, there is a more "open" sound because the notes of the chord have been spread out and are not stacked in thirds.

One concept that might save time when determining what voicing to use is to view part of the chord as a major or minor triad. For example, the second previously illustrated voicing is formed by playing a perfect fourth in the left hand and an F major chord in second inversion with the right.

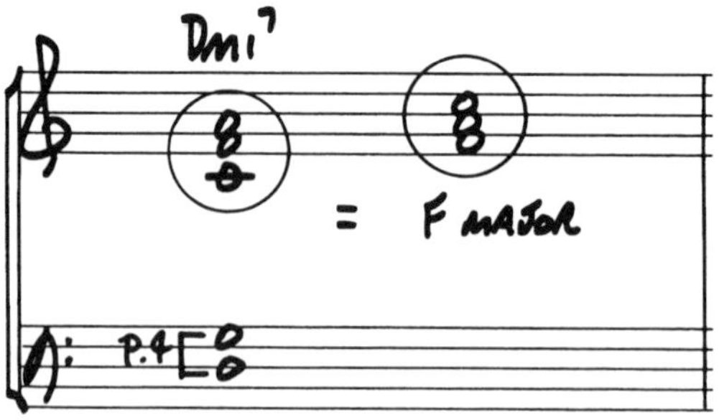

The knowledge of major and minor triads is always helpful when constructing chords. Even relatively advanced jazz chords can be partially analyzed as triads. Triads can serve as "building blocks" in most music theory.

Another characteristic of quartal harmony is that it lends itself to PARALLELISM. This is where the harmony shifts upwards or downwards with the intervals remaining the same.

When quartal harmony is used it is an example of an OPEN VOICING because the notes are spread apart. CLOSED VOICINGS imply notes that are separated by small intervals (primarily seconds). These types of voicings are just as useful as open voicings.

Again, notes are added to the basic chord (ninth, elevenths, and thirteenths). They can be placed close to each other to form a closed voicing.

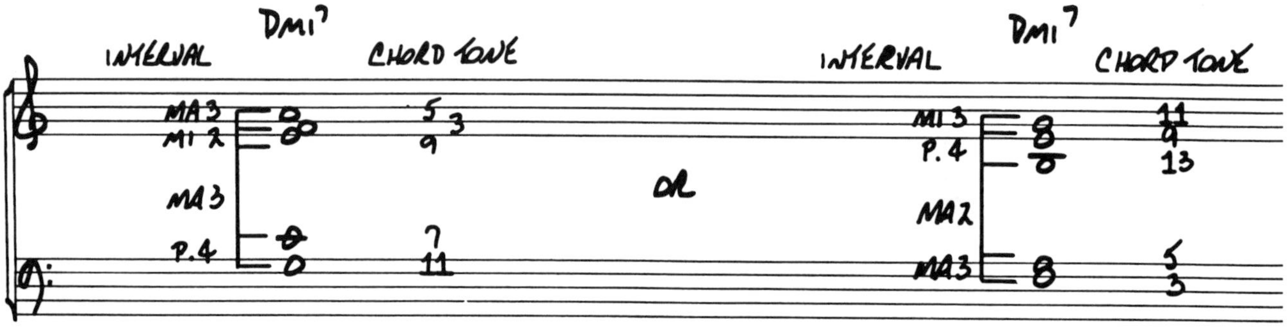

Open and closed voicings are incorporated in the following exercise. The two chords from "Illusions" are used. Feel free to create your own rhythms. Again, notes of long duration are used only for the purpose of illustration. Unless you are playing a ballad, percussive notes with some syncopation should be the norm.

EXERCISE 3

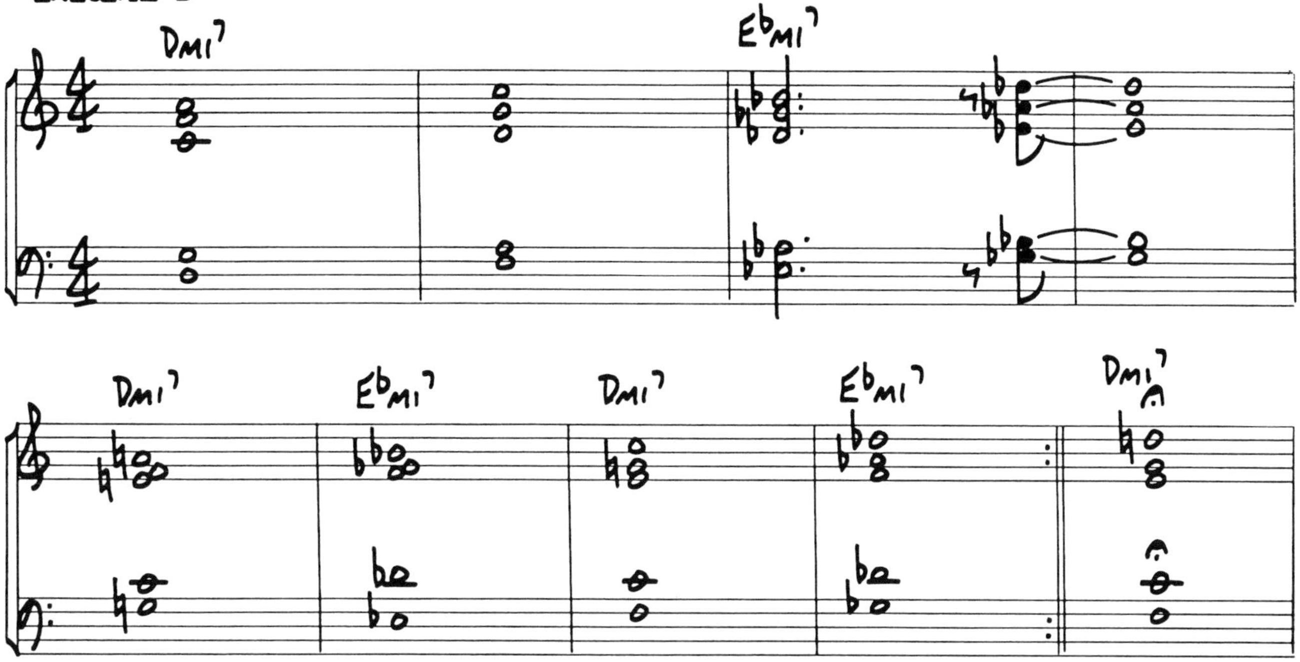

Piano comping concepts which were previously discussed are included in "Illusions": added notes, quartal harmony, parallelism, open and closed voicings. Do not feel limited to playing this example note-for note. A specific rhythm is included only for illustrative purposes. Each song sample will include fewer specified rhythms so you are free to improvise your own rhythm patterns. Eventually, you want to be able to look at the chord symbols and improvise an appropriate piano accompaniment (which is what jazz piano comping is all about). After you have played through the given piano part, look at the chord symbols and make up a piano part that sounds as authentic as possible.

*Illusions**

* All of the song examples in this book are recorded on Jamey Aebersold's play-a-long recording Volume 54, Maiden Voyage. See page 50 for more information.

BRIDGE
E♭MI7
DMI7
LAST X

As simple as this chord progression appears to be, it has been used for some well-known jazz pieces, including Miles Davis' "So What" from his Kind of Blue recording. (See the Index for the piece as recorded on Jamey Aebersold's Maiden Voyage.)

The form of this composition is AABA with each letter representing eight BARS (measures). The B section, which is an Eb minor seventh chord, is the bridge. As discussed previously, the bridge is a contrasting section that has a new chord progression or melody.

Many jazz compositions utilize a bridge to help with variety. As a jazz musician you are expected to "keep track of the bridge." This helps to make sure all of the musicians are at the same place at the same time. Challenge yourself to identify the bridge if it is included in the next jazz composition you hear or play.

Chapter 4: The Blues

When musicians refer to the BLUES they most often imply a 12-bar (twelve measures) chord progression which in its simplest form includes only three chords. All three chords are dominant sevenths. This chord progression can be repeated for as long as the musicians desire.

The pattern for 12-bar blues is as follows. Each Roman numeral represents one measure. This is the simplest form of the blues. *(for a detailed description of the blues refer to Chapter 2 of Jazz Piano Comping: From the Top)*

I7	I7	I7	I7
IV7	IV7	I7	I7
V7	IV7	I7	V7

If you play this chord progression at a quick tempo you will be playing a pattern for many songs of the 1950's. Songs like "Hound Dog," "Johnny B. Good," and "Good Golly Miss Molly" are a few examples of rock and roll songs that use a 12-bar Blues chord progression.

Bb Blues

As a jazz musician, you will will probably be asked to play the blues in keys such as Bb, F, or Eb. While guitarists and bassists often play the blues in A, E, or G, horn players (such as trumpeters or saxophonists) prefer keys using flats. Why is that?

This has to do with the fact that most wind players transpose on their instruments. If you are playing in the key of Bb, the trumpet player uses his or her key of C. Or if you are playing in Eb, the tenor saxophonist will be in F. Learn the blues in all keys and this will not be a problem.

"Don't Be Natural" is in the key of Bb. This is a very comfortable key for most horn players (especially beginners) so it will probably be one of the first you will be asked to use for the 12-Bar Blues. You will be using dominant chords based on the first (Bb), fourth (Eb), and fifth (F) chords of the key.

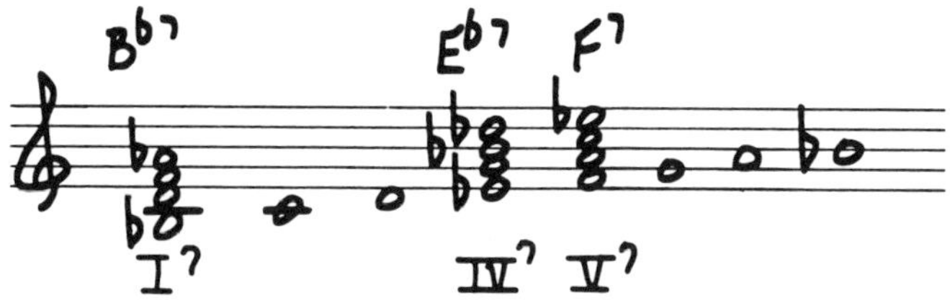

While each of these chords are harmonically correct, it would be "boring" to select them for voicings. Also, if you played each chord in root position the voice leading would sound disjointed because you "jump" from chord to chord. Two notes that are often added to a dominant voicing are the ninth and thirteenth. Remember, the ninth is the same pitch as the second and the thirteenth is the same as the sixth.

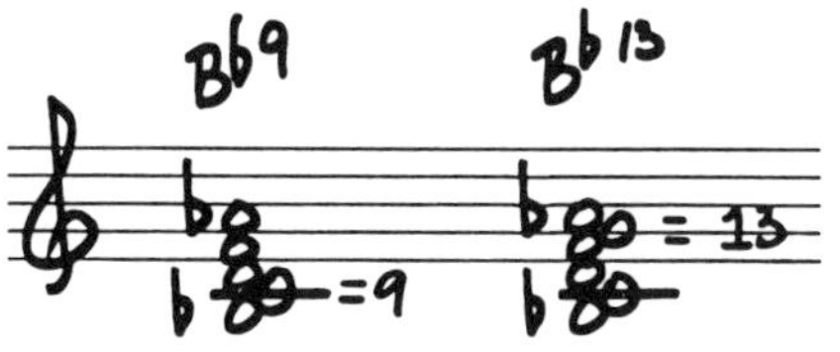

Again, just because a chord is harmonically correct does not always make it a good voicing. By spreading out the notes and using quartal harmony you can construct a chord that is correct <u>and</u> sounds good. Notice that the "important" notes are included in each voicing. Notes such as the root (to be played by the bassist) or fifth do not always have to be present.

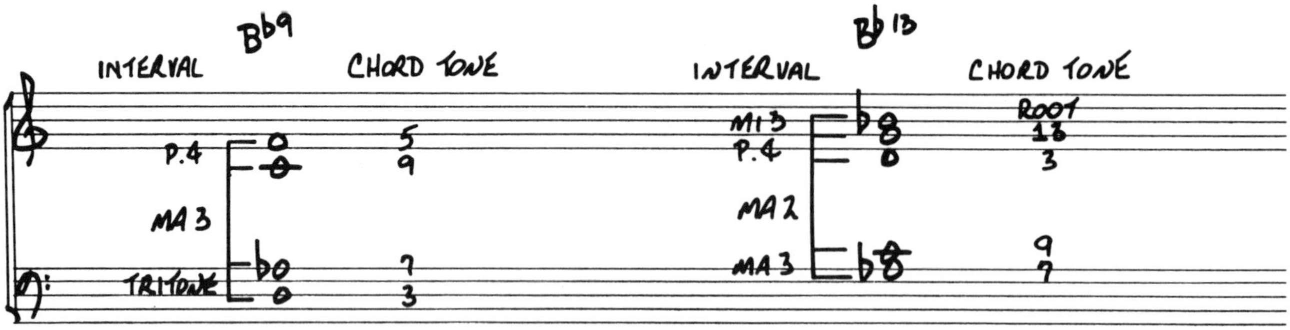

You are expected to add notes to create interesting jazz chords. Dominant seventh chords are indicated above the staff in the next exercise. The actual chords are listed below the suggested voicings. Eventually you should try to use these types of voicings whenever a dominant seventh chord is indicated. Dominant seventh chords work fine for rock and roll songs of the 1950's but they do not sound "authentic" for jazz compositions.

EXERCISE 4

Once you are comfortable moving from chord to chord, create your own rhythm. Initially you can repeat a rhythmic pattern from measure to measure. Try one of the following rhythms when comping this blues chord progression.

Then combine the different rhythms. Eventually you will improvise a rhythm that "fits." As always, listen to some accomplished jazz piano compers for rhythmic ideas.

One important quality that makes jazz harmony interesting is variety. You can create this by changing the voicings as well as adding pitches to the chord that is given.

Most jazz compositions do not have chord progressions that are stagnant. They usually move from chord to chord. This is one of the challenges to playing jazz chords but it can ultimately be very satisfying.

Look at the first four meaures of Exercise 4. They use the same chord (I7 in the key of Bb). These measueres need some variety to maintain the listeners' (and fellow musicians') interest. Play various voicings in those meaures to help "mix up" the sound of the chord progression.

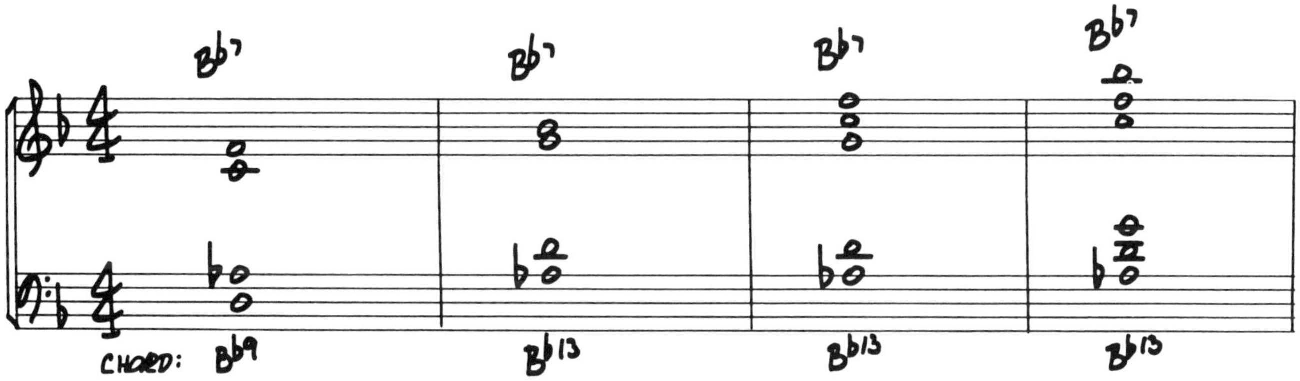

Use a different voicing every time the progression is repeated.

Another method for creating harmonic interest is to create a dissonance and then resolve it. You can do this in the first four meaures by raising the third of the chord (D) a half step to the fourth (Eb). Then resolve the harmonic tension by lowering the note back to the third.

The first chord would be a "sus4" because an Eb (the fourth note of the Bb scale) is played instead of D (the third note of the Bb scale). This harmonic resolution is very common in jazz as well as other types of compositions.

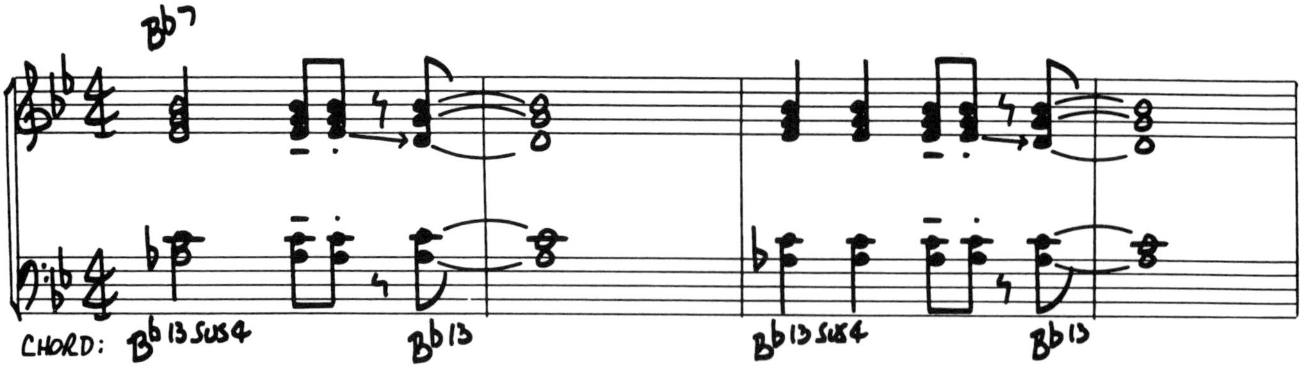

The only pitch that is changing from voicing to voicing is Eb (the fourth) to D (the third). Try creating this harmonic tension with the Eb7 chord (Ab to G) and F7 chord (Bb to A). A good amount of variety usually will be beneficial to your comping.

Here are some suggested voicings for "Don't be Natural." Feel free to create your own as well. Use percussive, syncopated rhythms most of the time. Also, add harmonic variety by using "sus4" chords which should resolve to dominant chords.

Don't Be Natural

F Blues

You need to be able to play the blues in any key. The next piece is in the key of F and is called the "Failing Grade Blues." Like Bb, the key of F is very popular with horn players (again, because of the transposition of their instruments).

If you play the 12-bar Blues in F using only dominant seventh chords based on the first (F), fourth (Bb), and fifth (C) notes of that key, you would use the following chords.

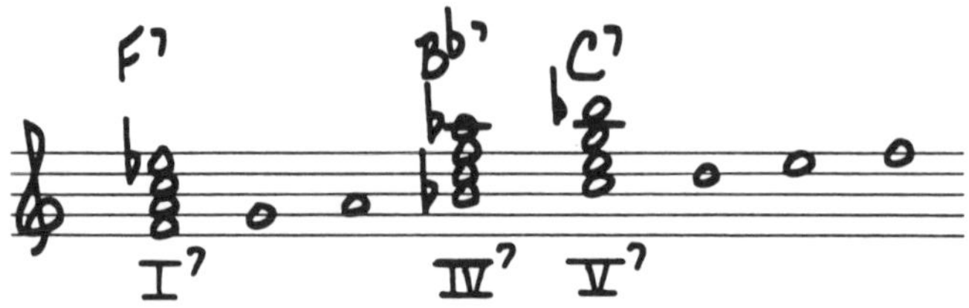

While these chords are useful for illustration, they would not be authentic jazz piano voicings. Notes have been added in the next exercise to the dominant seventh chords (ninths and thirteenths). This helps to create a more interesting chord progression. The actual chords are listed below the staff while the simpler chords are written above. Are you beginning to see the importance of adding notes to create jazz piano voicings?

Again, the "sus4" notes are indicated which can be played to help with the harmonic variety

Most jazz musicians want to progress beyond the simplest form of the 12-Bar Blues. They do this by adding chords to the progression. This is done with "Failing Grade Blues."

You have played all of the chord forms included in this piece. Now it is a matter of incorporating these chords into a 12-Bar Blues progression. While the `I7, IV7,` and `V7` chords are still an important part of the progression, they are not the only chords used.

Minor seventh going to dominant seventh chords are now included in the progression. This pattern will be discussed in detail in the next chapter.

One pattern is completed in one measure.

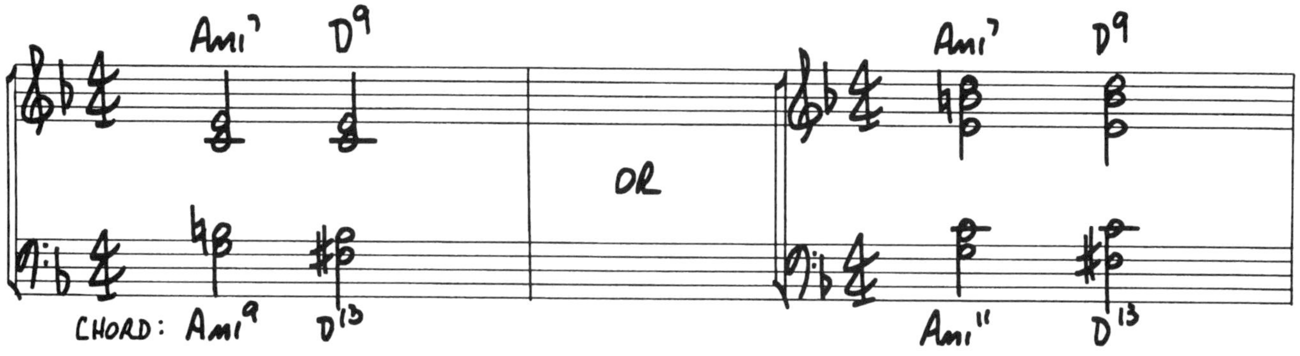

The other pattern is played in two measures. As you will see in the next chapter, the harmonic progression of a minor seventh to a dominant seventh chord is very common in jazz compositions.

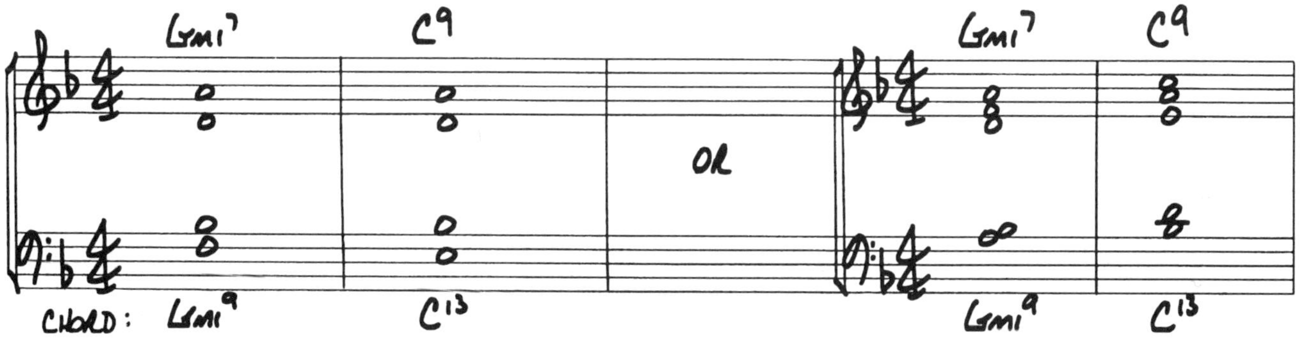

Here are some suggested voicings for each chord. As always, feel free to construct your own by interpreting the chord symbols.

The suggested voicings are followed by one possible interpretation. One of the joys (and challenges) of jazz piano comping is that there is no definitive rendition of an accompaniment. You should always try to improve by enhancing your harmonic vocabulary and creating interesting rhythms. These examples are provided as a means of showing you only one possibility.

Failing Grade Blues (version 1)

Failing Grade Blues (version 2)

Chapter 5: Playing Standards

A STANDARD is a piece of popular music that has "stood the test of time" and is still widely performed. It could be equated to the "classics" of classical music that remain popular year after year.

Standards are often part of a musical collection called a FAKE BOOK. Fake books contain compositions notated with melodies, chords, and lyrics if they can be sung. Most jazz musicians study the music in fake books because they include many of the pieces they will be asked to play.

A common practice for more advanced jazz musicians is to memorize the music and perform it at JAM SESSIONS. There they will play the melody (called the HEAD), improvise using the chord progression, and then play the melody once again before ending the piece. This type of performance is called a HEAD ARRANGEMENT because it is improvised at that time.

To become a respected jazz musician you must be able to play standards. When playing in a big band your music will probably be written out so that the large ensemble can play the appropriate music together. However, in an informal jam session you may only have a fake book or be asked to perform a piece from memory.

Most jazz compositions have chord progressions where the harmony changes quickly. With these types of pieces you can move rapidly from chord to chord and when done properly it will sound appropriate and authentic. There is a challenge any time the harmony becomes stagnant. This takes place if the same chord is to be played for a measure or more.

Often times a chord progression will remain on a major chord because it has the quality of being "stable." Try to add notes to the major triad to create harmonic interest. It is very rare that a triad will satisfy the harmonic requirement of a jazz composition. That is one of the reasons this style of music sounds so "lush."

If a C major chord is indicated you can add notes to it to create a fuller sound.

Each of these chords are "stacked" in thirds for purpose of illustration. Again, this type of construction is rarely used when creating jazz voicings.

Here are some voicings for each chord. Whenever possible, try to use an "open" sound which can be created with quartal harmony. Each note is in the chord, but they do not have to be in order (i.e. root-third-fifth-etc.).

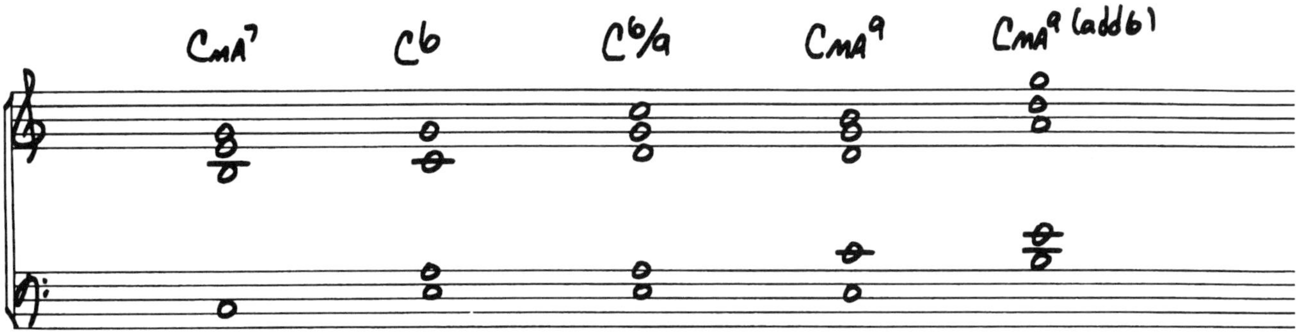

Each of these chords could be used if "C" is written above the staff as the chord symbol.

If that harmony was to be used for four measures you could alternate from chord to chord. Here the voicings are provided as well as the rhythm. Feel free to create your own comping once you have played this exercise.

The two chords from a key that are used most often in "Smooth Talker" are the second (`ii-7`) and fifth (`V7`). While this piece is in the key of C major the chord progression goes through several keys. As a jazz musician it is important to recognize the `ii-7` to `V7` chord pattern because it is so widely used.

The first two measures of this piece are the `ii-7` to `V7` chords in the key of C major. They are Dmin7 and G7, respectively.

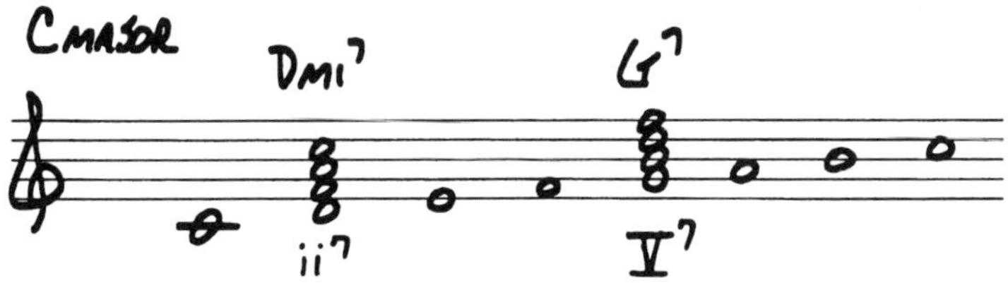

You can add notes to these chords to create a more interesting harmony. Choose voicings that utilize smooth voice leading. By changing one note you can move from the `ii-7` to `V7` chord in any key. You can create the rhythm on your own in this exercise.

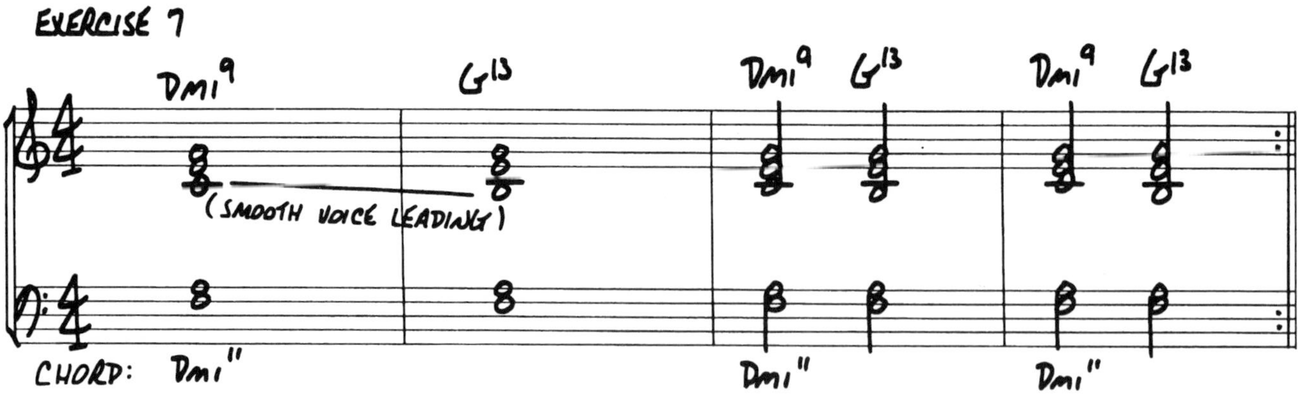

The third and fourth measure of "Smooth Talker" are the second (`ii-7`) and fifth (`V7`) chords of D major. An Emin7 is the second chord of that key and an A7 is the fifth chord.

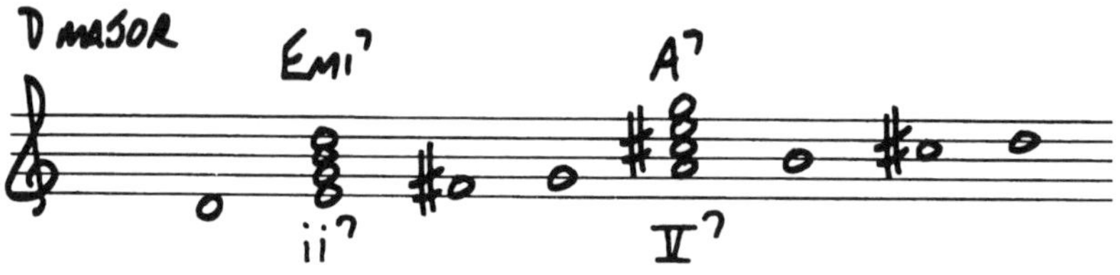

A Minor ninth chord can replace a minor seventh chord. A ninth or thirteenth chord can be substituted for a dominant seventh chord. They can represent the second (`ii-7`) and fifth (`V7`) chords of a major key. Again, create your own rhythm.

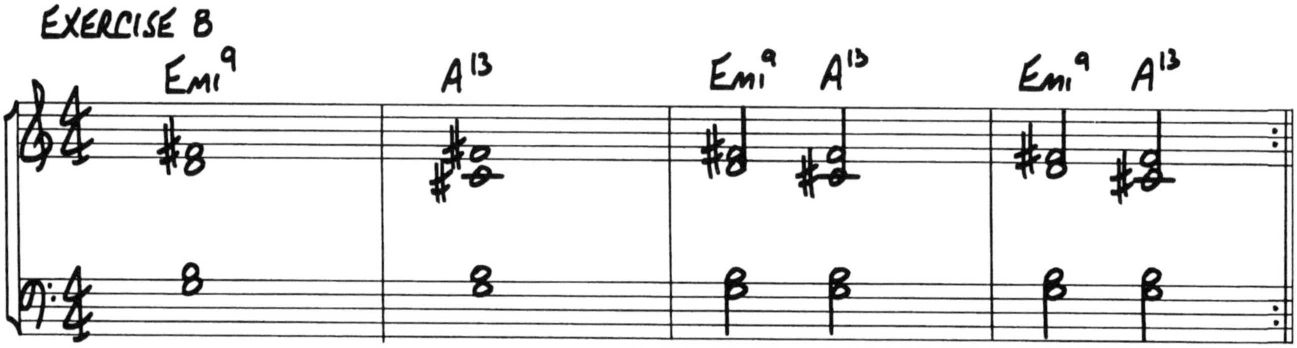

Did you notice only one note is changing from chord to chord (D to C#)? Always play with as smooth of voice leading as possible.

Here are the other `ii-7` and `V7` chords used in "Smooth Talker" and their corresponding keys. You should soon see how common it is for chords to move from `ii-7` to `V7` in jazz compositions.

The form of "Smooth Talker" is AABA with each letter representing eight bars. This is another example of this common song form used in jazz. Again, the "B" represents the bridge which has a different set of chords than the "A" section.

Play the Coda the last time through the progression. Create your own rhythms using the voicings provided or ones that you form by interpreting the chord symbols.

Smooth Talker

MODERATE SWING (♩ = 102)

G13
Dmi9
G13
Emi9
A13
Ami9
D13
Abmi9
Db13
TO CODA
CMA9
F9
Emi9
A13
C6/9
F13
Emi11
REPEAT AS DESIRED
TAKE CODA LAST X
CMA9
CMA9
C6/9
C6/9

Chapter 6: Straight Eighth Notes

Most pieces you will play in a jazz setting will have "swing" or uneven eighth notes. That is the rhythm pattern that often defines whether a composition is considered jazz or not.

Whenever you see words such as "Latin," "Bossa," or "Even 8ths" to describe the rhythmic feel, eighth notes will be of equal length.

The BOSSA NOVA is a style of music or a dance of Brazilian origin. As discussed previously, it can be labelled as a "Bossa" at the beginning of the piece. Your primary concern is to play the eighth notes evenly.

When playing a Latin piece use notes of short duration as well as much syncopation. The rhythm of this style of music is one of its most appealing qualities.

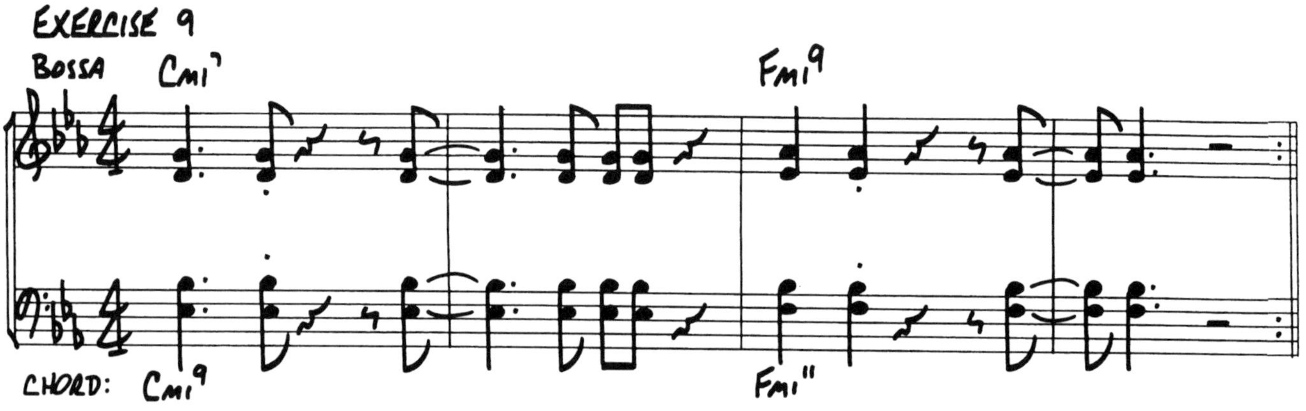

The percussive quality of the piano is an asset when playing this style of music. Use the sustain pedal sparingly when comping for Bossas. This is one type of rhythm that you could use when playing "Your Bossa Wantsa You."

Two chords are included in this piece which are dissonant in nature. They add to its interesting and varied harmonic flavor. The first is a HALF-DIMINISHED chord (sometimes called a minor seventh flat five chord). Here it is illustrated as a stack of minor and major thirds. Each interval is a minor third except from the fifth to the seventh which is a major third.

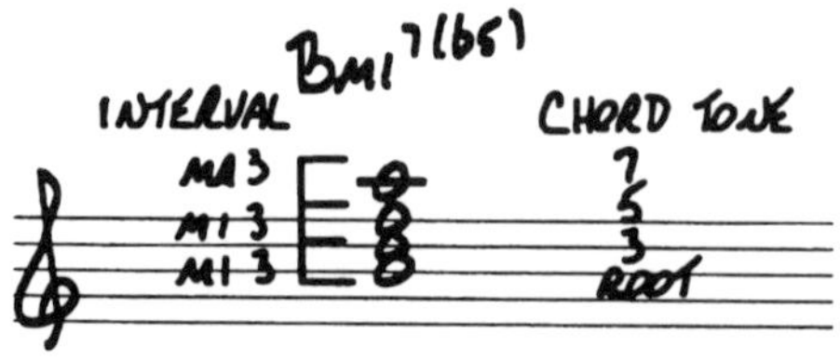

The chord symbol for this chord is a letter representing the root followed by "ø7," "-7b5," or "mi7b5," or "m7-5."

Bø7 B-7b5 Bmi7b5 Bm7-5

It is important to notice if there is a diagonal line through the circle. If it is not there then the chord represents a DIMINISHED SEVENTH chord.

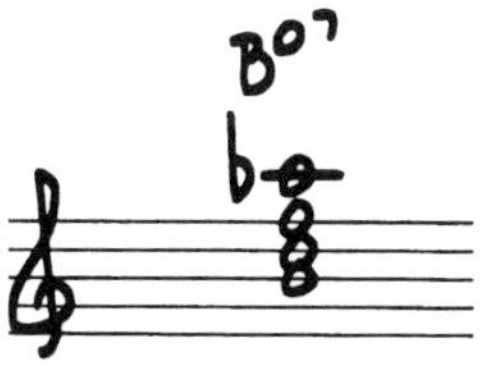

This is a chord which has only minor thirds (three half steps) for the intervals between the notes.

By rearranging the notes of a half-diminished chord you can play it with an "open" sound.

A tritone is the interval between the bottom two notes and a perfect fourth separates the top two. Each note is part of a D half-diminished chord.

As with most jazz chords, you can add notes to create a more "authentic" jazz sound. Two notes that can be added to a half-diminished chord are the eleventh and flatted thirteenth. If the root is D, those notes would be G and Bb, respectively. (Remember, an eleventh is the same as the fourth and a thirteenth is the same as the sixth.)

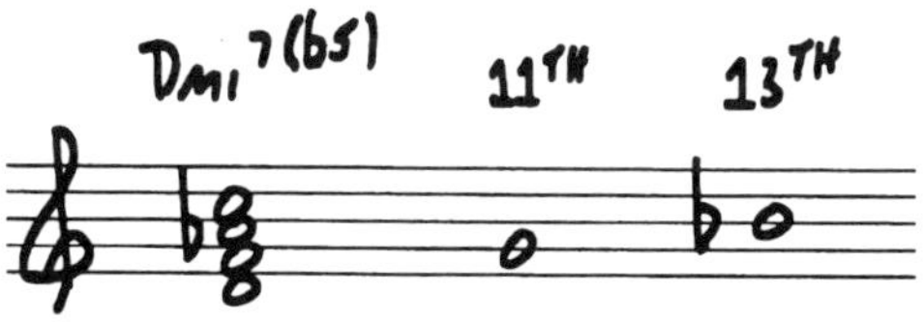

By adding those notes to a voicing you can create even more dissonance. This makes the harmonic resolution which usually follows even more "satisfying" to the listener.

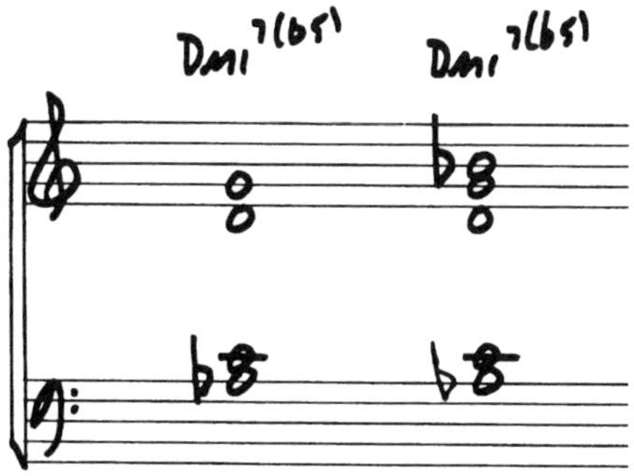

The other dissonant chord is a DOMINANT SEVENTH SHARPED NINTH which has one note (the raised ninth) added to a dominant seventh chord. This note is sometimes written as a flatted tenth in jazz arrangements. Both chord spellings will sound the same.

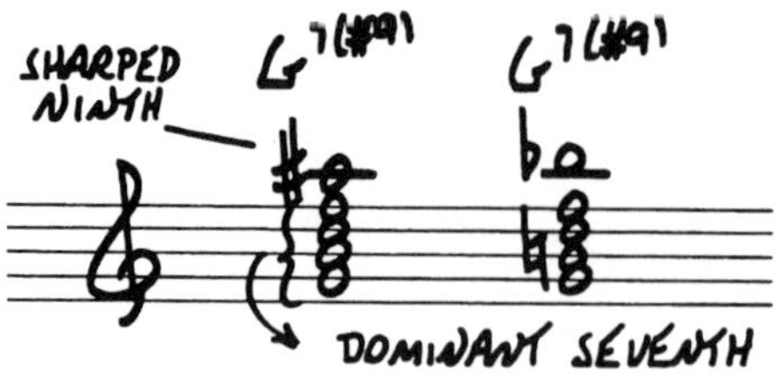

Make sure whenever you see the second voicing that the third of the chord is still four half steps above the root and the raised ninth is three half steps above the root's octave. It is the dissonance of these two notes that gives this chord its "bite."

The chord symbol for a dominant seventh sharped ninth chord is a letter representing the root followed by "7+9" or "7#9."

G7+9 G7#9

A note that is commonly added to a dominant seventh sharped ninth chord is the flatted thirteenth. If the chord is based on G7, that note will be Eb.

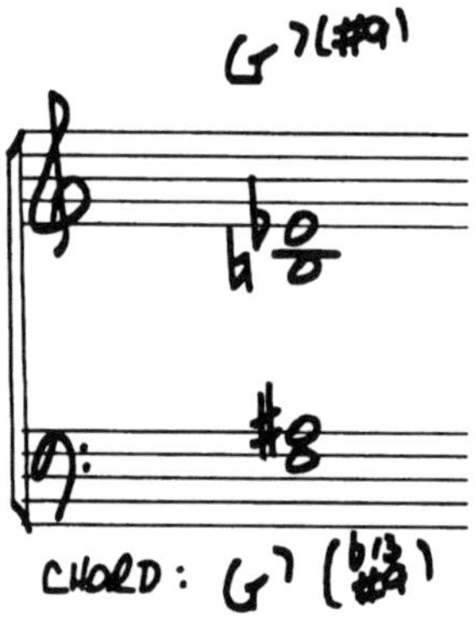

Another voicing of this chord is a good example of a polychord. The Eb major triad is stacked above a G dominant seventh chord. A relatively complicated jazz chord can be thought of as a combination of two simpler chords.

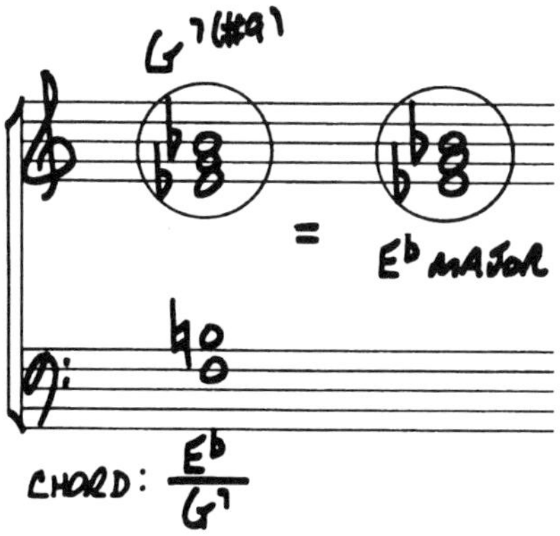

Use a Latin-style rhythm when playing the following exercise. Even eighth notes are to be used. A suggested rhythmic pattern is notated in the first two measures. You supply the rhythm in the last two measures. Notes have been added to the chords to create even more harmonic tension.

Can you find the second (`ii-7`) to fifth (`V7`) chords in the next song sample? They are in the ninth and tenth measures where Eb-7 goes to Ab9.

This pattern resolves to the first chord (`IΔ7`) of the key (Db major) in the eleventh and twelfth measures.

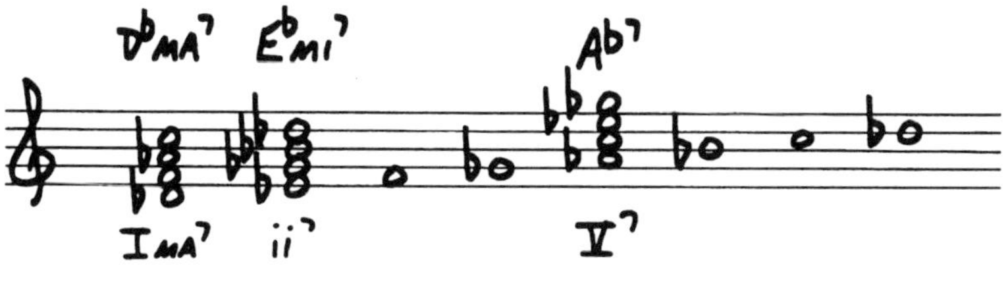

The chord progression is in that key for only those four measures. It is in C minor for the other twelve.

Create your own rhythms when playing the suggested voicings for "Your Bossa Wantsa You." Feel free to leave "space" between the notes of the rhythm. Latin rhythms are created by playing "on the beat" as well as off (syncopation). The phrase "less is more" can be applied to the comping pattern used for this style of music. Feel free to use repetition as well when creating the rhythm. It helps to build the intensity of the accompaniment.

Your Bossa Wantsa You

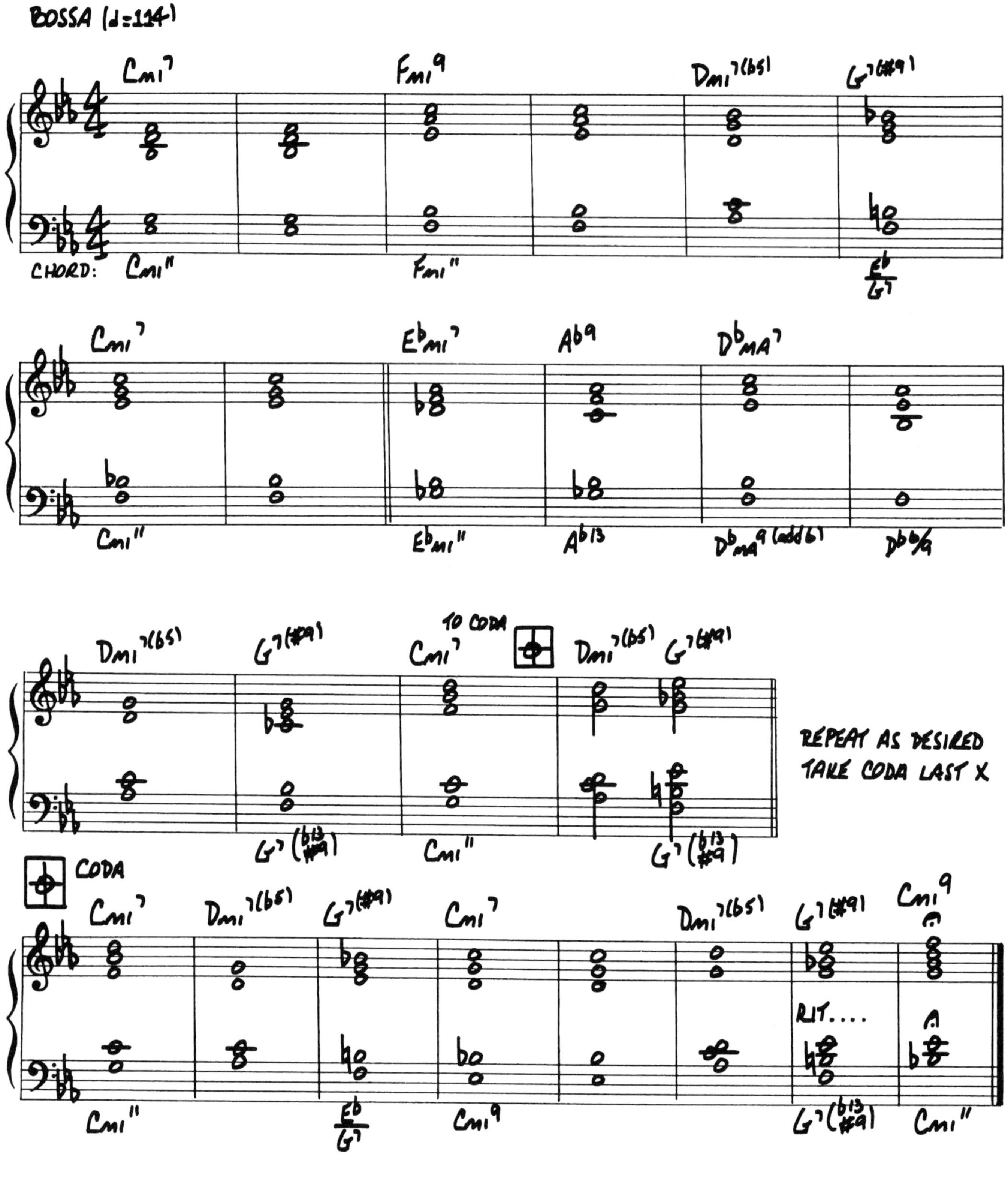

Chapter 7: More Advanced Harmony

The study of jazz harmony can be a lifelong endeavor which is one of the joys of this music. If you learn the material in a step-by-step fashion, it can "make sense" and you will continue to grow as a musician.

Many beginners can find jazz harmony frustrating because of the complexity of the chords. Often times it is one of their first attempts at interpreting chord symbols. If you understand the significance of each part of a chord symbol and know the "important" notes, you should be able to do well in most jazz ensembles.

You have already seen most of the chord types used in "Back to School." The majority of the chord progression is a series of second and fifth chords in major and minor keys. Again, if you can recognize this relationship it will be of help to you when working with many jazz chord progressions.

The two new chord types are MINOR SIXTH and DOMINANT SEVENTH FLATTED NINTH chords. Are you beginning to understand the construction of chords just by looking at their names?

A minor sixth chord is formed by adding the sixth note of a scale to a minor triad.

The chord symbol is similar to a minor seventh chord except a "6" is used instead of a "7."

G-6   Gm6   Gmi6   Gmin6

All of these chord symbols represent the same chord.

Here are some possible chord voicings for a G minor sixth chord.

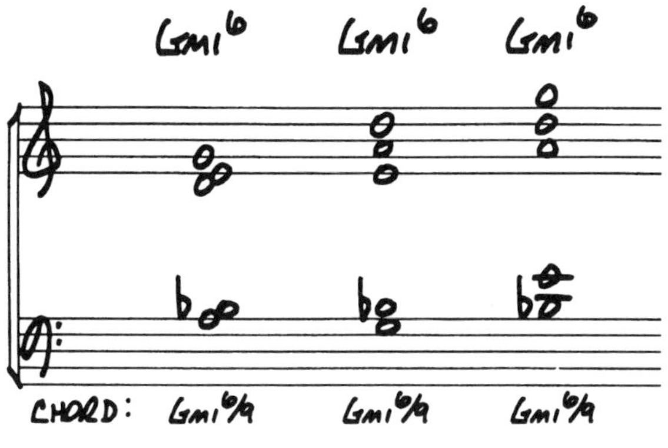

Alternate between a G minor seventh chord and a G minor sixth. Do you see the seventh (F) is shifted down one half step to become the sixth (E)? This shifting of the harmony can usually be used if a minor chord is to be played for an extended period of time.

The other new chord type used in "Back to School" is a DOMINANT SEVENTH FLATTED NINTH chord. As the name implies, a note - the flatted ninth - of a scale is added to a dominant seventh chord.

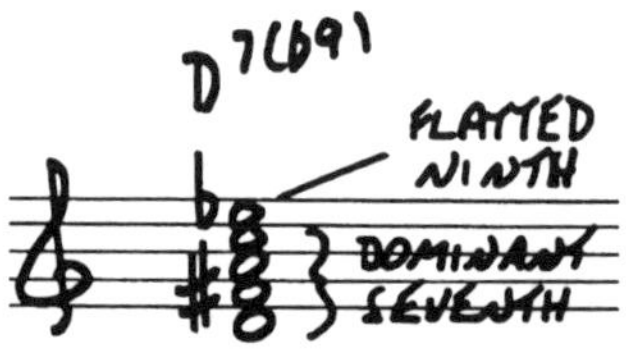

The chord symbol for a dominant seventh flatted ninth chord is similar to a dominant seventh sharped ninth chord except a "-" or "b" is used instead of a "+" or "#."

D7-9 D7b9

Here are some voicings for a D dominant seventh flatted ninth chord. Again, notes have been added to create even more dissonance. One quality of dominant chords is "harmonic unrest." The dissonance of notes such as the flatted ninth add to this characteristic.

You can often substitute a dominant seventh flatted ninth chord for a dominant seventh sharped ninth chord and vice versa. Try playing either chord when a dominant seventh sharped ninth or flatted ninth appears in the next song sample.

One element of jazz harmony that may become a factor in a jam session is TRITONE SUBSTITUTION. This concept can be used with dominant chords. If you look at two dominant seventh chords a tritone (three whole steps) apart, you can see there are two notes in common.

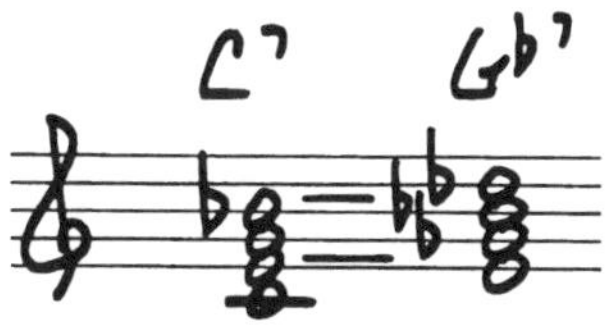

The third of C7 (E) is also the seventh of Gb7 and the seventh of C7 (Bb) is the third of Gb7.

Therefore, if a dominant chord built on C is indicated you can usually substitute a Gb dominant chord for it. This can be done by the bassist changing to the appropriate note.

Tritone substitution can sometimes be used to create a smoother chord movement. For instance in "Back to School" there is a series of three chords: G-7 to C7+9 to F-9.

EXERCISE 12

By replacing C7+9 with Gb9 (its tritone substitute) you move smoothly from chord to chord by half steps. The only change being made is the bass note (which is in parentheses) of the second chord. You do not even have to change your voicing to achieve a tritone substitution.

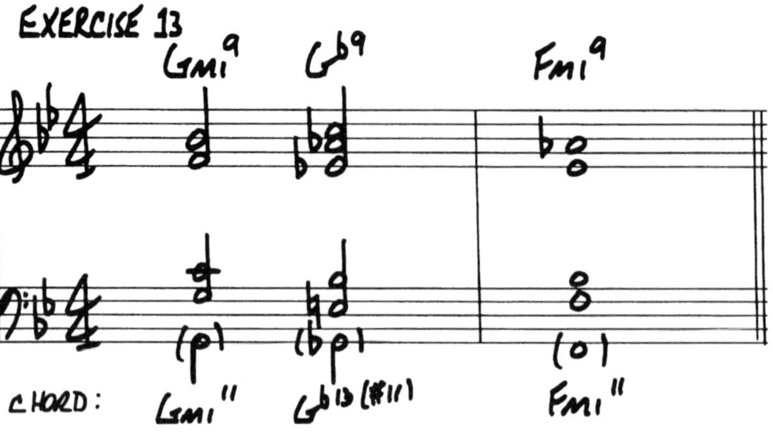

Some tritone substitutions are written below the staff in "Back to School." They offer an alternative chord progression. Remember, this harmonic rule only works for dominant chords and does not always sound "right." The bass movement is usually controlled by the bassist who will decide when tritone substitutions are to be used.

Another way to create variety is to change the duration of the notes when comping. When using half notes, the chords will be played twice in each measure.

If the bassist plays with the same sense of rhythm you are creating a TWO BEAT feel. It is called that because you are playing on two of the beats (the first and third) in each measure. The bassist will be playing primarily the root and fifth of each chord.

When he or she starts to play quarter notes (called a WALKING BASS line) you support that rhythm by playing syncopated figures.

EXERCISE 15

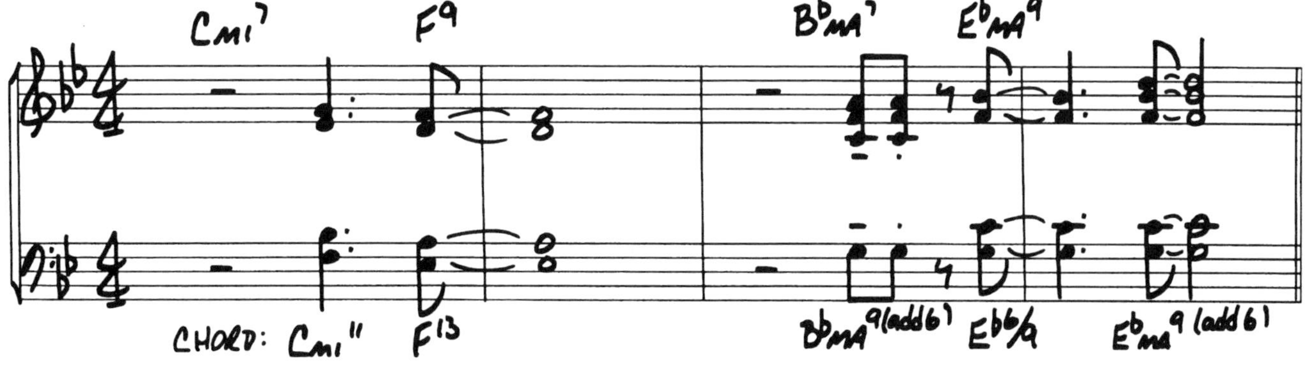

Use a two beat feel the first time through the chord progression of "Back to School." Switch to syncopated rhythms after the first time through the piece. If you are playing with a bassist make sure he or she understands both feels and that you both are in "sync."

Back to School

Cmi7
F9
B♭ma7
E♭ma9
Ami7(♭5)
D7(#9)
Gmi7
C7(#9)
Fmi9
B♭13
G♭9
E9
E♭9
Ami7(♭5)
D7(#9)
Gmi7
TO CODA
(G7(#9))
A♭13
SOLO BREAK (1ST X ONLY)
CODA
Emi7(♭5)
Ami7(♭5)
D7(#9)
Gmi7
Emi7(♭5)
Ami7(♭5)
D7(#9)
Gmi9

Chapter 8: Modal Playing

MODES are a selection of notes arranged as a scale that form a tonal center. Diatonic (church) modes begin and end on various notes of a major scale. Each note of a major scale is the beginning of a mode.

Note of Major Scale	Mode
1st	Ionian
2nd	Dorian
3rd	Phrygian
4th	Lydian
5th	Mixolydian
6th	Aeolian
7th	Locrian

Here are the seven modes based on G major.

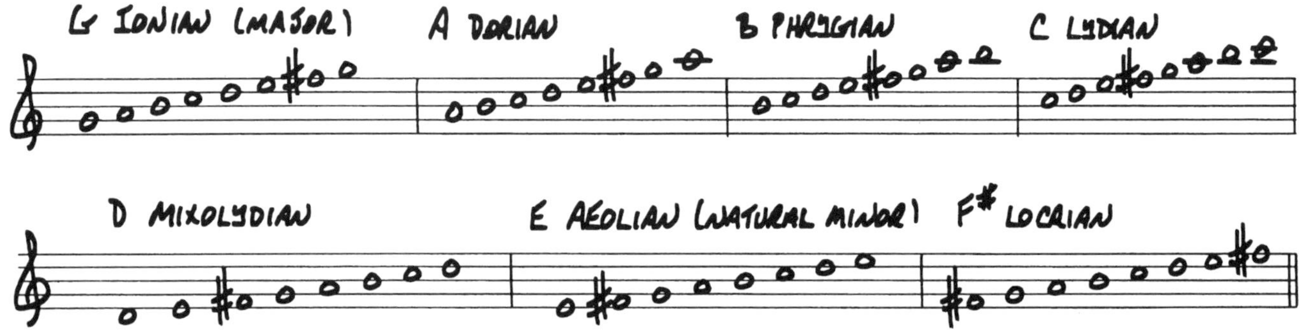

As you can see, each of these modes are the notes of a G major scale starting on various pitches of that scale.

MODAL JAZZ was a type of composition developed in the late 1950's. Miles Davis' Kind of Blue album featured pieces based on various modes. Jazz musicians such as John Coltrane and Herbie Hancock also wrote pieces and improvised in this genre.

An important mode used when improvising on some of these pieces is DORIAN which is the second mode of a major key. The notes of this mode are from a G major scale but have an A minor quality to the tonal center. You can use the notes of the G major scale when improvising in A dorian.

The chord played for this mode is A minor seventh.

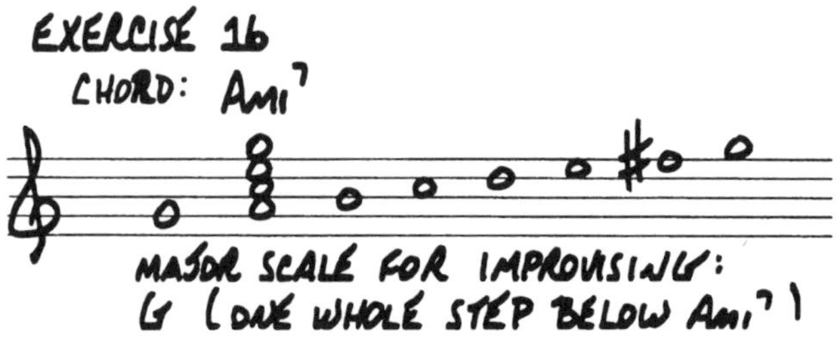

Various dorian modes are used in "First Ripple." ("Illusions" is also based on two dorian modes, D dorian and Eb dorian.) You can view these chords as the second (`ii-7`) chord of a major key. Play the major scale one step below each minor chord and you will be using the appropriate dorian mode.

Most chord symbols in "First Ripple" have two parts. These are called SLASH CHORDS or CHORDS WITH ALTERED ROOTS. The information to the left of the diagonal line is the chord while the letter to the right is the bass note.

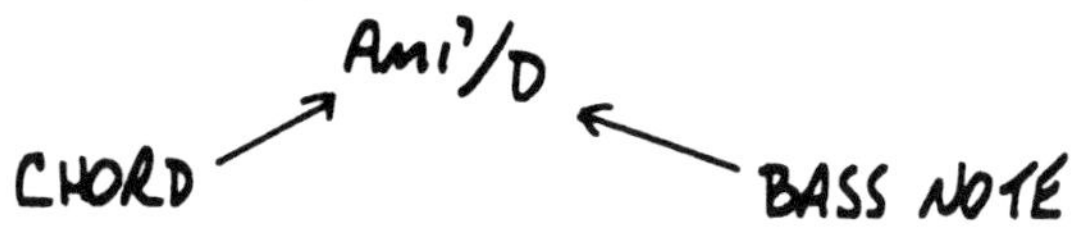

It is the responsibility of the bassist to play the note on the right. You are to play the notes of the chord and any pitches in the lower register should be the altered bass note.

Another way the chords in "First Ripple" could be notated are with DOMINANT SEVENTH SUSPENDED FOURTH chord symbols. A suspended ("sus") chord implies that one of the notes is raised. In this case the third of the chord is raised by one half step to become the fourth.

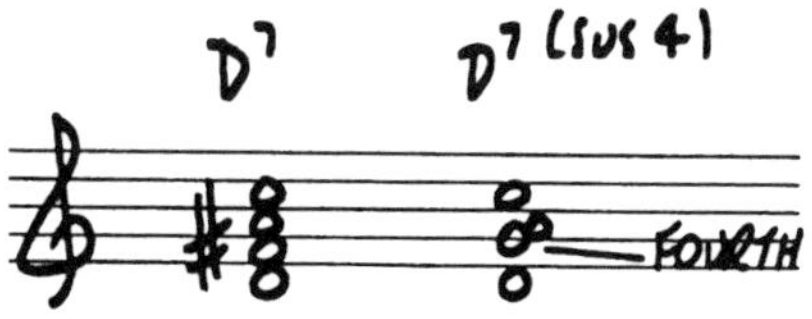

The slash chords could also be ninth chords with suspended fourths. Both chord symbols represent the same chords.

A-7/D = D9sus4

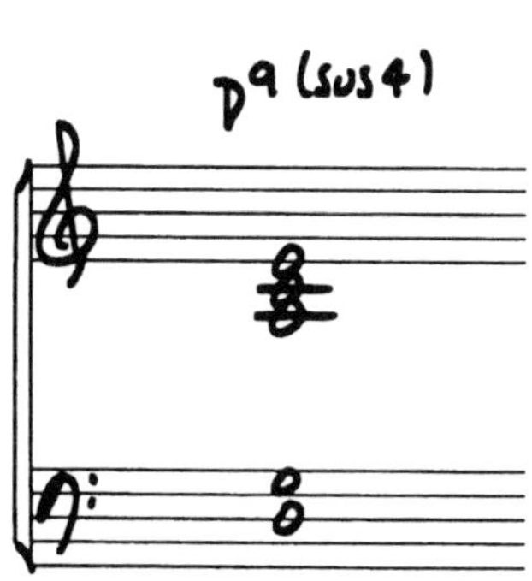

As a jazz musician you must be able to interpret a variety of chord symbols that can represent the same thing.

The first time through the chord progression of "First Ripple" you are to play a certain rhythm.

This is an example of SYNCOPATION where a chord (or note) is played when it is not expected (on the "weak" part of the measure).

When playing syncopation (which is very common in jazz) you may want to keep track of your foot movement which can tap to the beat. Pay attention if a note occurs on the UPBEAT (when your foot is up) or the DOWNBEAT (in this case when your foot is down).

For instance, the rhythm for the chords in “First Ripple” could be viewed like this. The arrows pointing up indicate when the chord is played on the upbeat and the downward arrows represent a downbeat.

This system can be of help when playing the interesting rhythms of jazz (as well as other styles).

“First Ripple” has an AABA form with “B” once again representing the bridge. Use the suggested rhythm which was previously illustrated the first time through. On the CHORUSES (sets of chord progressions) that follow, improvise your own rhythm. One possible interpretation of the chords has been provided. Feel free to deviate from it once you are familiar with the chords.

You can let the chords ring for an extended period of time if desired. Do this by depressing the notes for a long duration or by using the sustain pedal. If you play this piece with a rhythm section, listen to each other for rhythmic ideas. Straight eighth notes are indicated so use them for the basic pulse.

First Ripple

BRIDGE:
Bbmi7/Eb (Eb7SUS4)
C#mi9
Ami7/D (D7SUS4)
Cmi7/F (F7SUS4)

APPENDIX

CORRESPONDING RECORDING

As discussed previously, the chord progressions of the song samples are recorded on Volume 54 of Jamey Aebersold's play-a-long recording, Maiden Voyage.

Here are the pieces that correspond to the ones from this book:

Interm. Jazz Piano Comping	**Maiden Voyage**
Illusions	Impressions
Don't Be Natural	Bb Blues ("Shuffle-Time")
Failing Grade Blues	F Blues ("Tootsie")
Smooth Talker	Satin Doll
Your Bossa Wantsa You	Blue Bossa
Back to School	Autumn Leaves
First Ripple	Maiden Voyage

The Aebersold recordings are recorded in such a way that the bass and drums are on one stereo channel while piano and drums are on the other. You can practice with piano and drums only to create your own "jazz trio."

For further study you may want to obtain Jazz Piano Voicings: Transcribed Comping from Volume 54 'Maiden Voyage'. A detailed transcription of Jamey Aebersold's piano part is illustrated. This is an excellent resource to see how jazz piano comping can be developed and varied.

The book and recordings are available from your local music store or from:

Jamey Aebersold
P. O. Box 1244
New Albany, IN 47151-1244
1-800-456-1388

GLOSSARY

Bars - A term to describe measures (12-Bar Blues, for example).

Blues - A type of music usually with a chord progression twelve measures (bars) in length. In its simplest form only three chords (I7, IV7, V7) are used.

Bossa Nova - A style of music originating in Brazil that has even eighth notes.

Bridge - A contrasting section (B) which has a new set of chords and/or melody in comparison to the first section (A).

Chart - A term used for "jazz composition."

Chord - Three or more notes played at the same time.

Chord Progression - A series of chords played one after another.

Chord Symbols - A set of letters and numbers written above the staff which indicate what chords are to be played.

Chorus - One time through a chord progression.

Dorian - The mode based on the second note of a major scale.

Fake Book - A music book that uses only melodies, chords and sometimes lyrics for notation.

Head - The melody of a jazz composition.

Head Arrangement - A performance of a piece that is not pre-planned. The form is usually the melody, improvisation on the chord progression and then the melody is played with some sort of ending.

Jam Session - An informal performance featuring primarily the improvisation of jazz standards.

Modal Jazz - A style of music developed in the late 1950's where compositions were based on various modes.

Mode - An eight-note scale based on pitches from a major scale.

Parallelism - Harmony shifts upwards or downwards with most of the intervals remaining the same.

Quartal Harmony - Chords are constructed primarily by intervals of a fourth.

Root - The note on which a chord is based.

Scale - A series of pitches played one at a time that are usually a half step or whole step apart.

Slash Chords - A chord that has a note other than the root as its lowest pitch. The chord symbol represents the chord on the left of a diagonal line and the bass note to the right.

Standard - A piece of music that remains popular and can be used for jazz arrangements and improvisation.

Swing Eighth Notes - Eighth notes performed in an uneven fashion. The first note in a set of two is longer than the second.

Syncopation - Playing a note or chord where it is not expected (on the "weak" part of the measure).

Tertian Harmony - Chords are constructed by intervals of a third.

Triad - A three-note chord.

Tritone - An interval of three whole steps.

Tritone Substitution - Dominant chords a tritone apart can be played for one another.

Two Beat - The accent is on the first and third beats of the measure. Play primarily the root and fifth of each chord.

Walking Bass - A series of notes played by the bassist usually one beat in length that outline the harmony.